$2

WILD FIBONACCI

Nature's Secret Code Revealed

by Joy N. Hulme

Illustrations by
Carol Schwartz

TRICYCLE PRESS
BERKELEY | TORONTO

Dear Reader,

How do we know about the number code evident in the lifesaving features of many animals? The man who discovered it was a brilliant mathematician who lived in Pisa, Italy, about the same time as the construction of the famous leaning tower. He was known as Leonardo da Pisa, and in 1202 he published a book called *Liber Abaci* that told about a fascinating sequence of numbers. Because he used the pen name Fibonacci, the pattern became known as the "Fibonacci sequence" and each number is called a "Fibonacci number." The next number in the sequence comes from adding the two numbers before it (1, 1, 2, 3, 5, 8, 13, 21, 34, 55, 89, and so on).

A curve called an "equiangular spiral" can be plotted using Fibonacci squares (1 x 1, 2 x 2, 3 x 3, 5 x 5, and so on). They are arranged clockwise in sequential order (see the diagram on the following pages), and an arc is drawn connecting opposite corners until a spiral is formed. The curve can continue forever without ever becoming completely straight.

Many animal horns, claws, beaks, teeth, talons, tusks, and shells, such as those found in this book, are curved to fit the spiral. Some are tight curves, like the center of a shell. Others curve more gradually, but each shape fits a portion of the equiangular spiral. Even human teeth curve enough to make a match.

Long before Leonardo da Pisa lived, great artists and architects recognized the amazing beauty of a special shape known as the "golden rectangle." The proportions of this rectangle are more pleasing to the eye than longer, narrower rectangles or shorter, fatter ones. The length of the short and long sides are related to each other in the same way as two adjacent Fibonacci numbers (2 to 3, 3 to 5, 5 to 8, and so on). To find the measurement of the long side, the length of the short side is multiplied by 1.62. The book you're reading was designed with this proportion in mind (10.5 inches x 1.62 = 17 inches). Measure the open pages and see for yourself.

Ways to have fun with Fibonacci

Count the number of needles in a pine needle bundle (1, 2, 3, or 5) or the number of petals on a flower. Many blooms have five petals: buttercups, pansies, violets, hibiscus, geraniums, primroses, apples, pears, apricots, berries, cherries, squash, cucumbers, and so on. Cosmos have eight petals, and daisies have 13, 21, 34, 55, or 89 depending on the variety. The number of sections in seedpods are often Fibonacci numbers. Notice how the bracts on palm trees, artichokes, pineapples, and pinecones spiral in two directions. In each case, the number of spirals is one Fibonacci number one way and the next number in the sequence the other way.

Check out how the leaves on corn plants, pussy willows, and many trees are arranged in a spiral around the stem so that none of the leaves shade the ones directly below from the sunlight they need to grow. Look for equiangular spirals on shells, opening fern fronds, ocean waves, mature sunflower heads, and animal features like those in this book. Examine art books and identify how the golden proportion is applied. You'll find the Fibonacci sequence all around you—a vital element in nature's grand design.

In the Fibonacci sequence
each new number comes
from adding up the two before
and figuring the sum.

This number set is used to plot
a graceful curving line
that's often found in nature
as part of its design.

Fibonacci creatures
have a certain body part
which fits the winding, coiling shape
that spirals on this chart.

These parts are most important
to help the beasts survive.
Finding food and fighting foes
can keep each one alive.

One walrus dives in arctic seas
and swims with flippered feet.
Stiff whiskers on her upper lip
find snails and clams to eat.

Her long curved **tusks** are useful
to a body big and stout.
They jab into an icy chunk
and help her climb right out.

1

One elephant will wave his ears
like fans to keep him cool
or squirt a shower with his trunk
in some deep jungle pool.

His ivory **tusks** are handy tools
to strip the bark from trees,
to dig up roots for tasty treats,
or fight fierce enemies.

1

One parrot has a scarlet **beak**,
and sports a feathered vest.
One bird is white from top to tail
and wears a yellow crest.

Two curving **beaks** are shaped just right
to gobble food all day.
They crack the shells of nuts and seeds
and toss the hulls away.

1 + 1 = 2

One crocodile lives in a marsh
and lays soft speckled eggs.
Two alligators walk about
on short and stocky legs.

Three reptiles have fierce curving **teeth**
to snatch a bite to eat.
They drown the prey, twist it apart,
and gulp the chunks of meat.

1 + 2 = 3

Two eagles glide high in the sky,
and float above the breeze.
Three red-tailed hawks spread pointed wings
to fly with equal ease.

Five birds of prey, like bullets,
drop down with deadly aim.
Their curving **talons** grab a meal
and carry off the game.

2 + 3 = 5

Three leopards have soft golden fur
with brown rosette designs.
Five tigers' coats are orange,
striped with jet-black lines.

Eight jungle cats will stalk their prey
on quiet padded paws,
then quickly pounce to capture it
with sharp and curling **claws**.

3 + 5 = 8

Five bighorns race with speed and grace,
sure-footed on the rocks.
Eight plunge down steep and rough terrain,
foot pads absorbing shocks.

Thirteen Rocky Mountain sheep
have **horns** that look like snails.
These mating-time head-butting tools
are only used by males.

5 + 8 = 13

Eight hippos swim and soak and rest
submerged up to their eyes.
Thirteen others doze and yawn
beneath blue sun-kissed skies.

Twenty-one with curving **tusks**
might fight along the bank.
Sometimes they face off jaw to jaw
and sometimes head to flank.

8 + 13 = 21

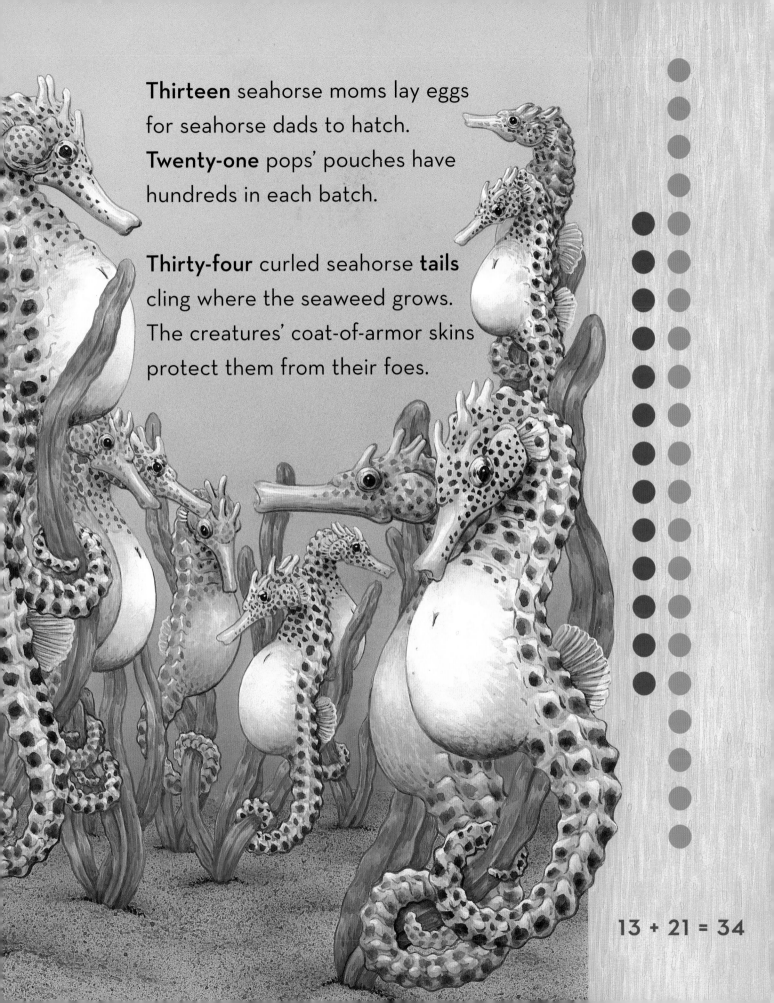

Thirteen seahorse moms lay eggs
for seahorse dads to hatch.
Twenty-one pops' pouches have
hundreds in each batch.

Thirty-four curled seahorse **tails**
cling where the seaweed grows.
The creatures' coat-of-armor skins
protect them from their foes.

13 + 21 = 34

Twenty-one white ibises
roost high up in the trees.
Thirty-four wade in the marsh
in water to their knees.

Fifty-five long curving bills can
build a nest of sticks,
scoop a marshy meal to eat,
or feed new baby chicks.

21 + 34 = 55

Thirty-four brown sundial shells have washed up on the beach. Fifty-five striped auger twists are found in easy reach.

Eighty-nine are ocean homes where soft sea creatures dwell, well protected when they hide inside a sturdy shell.

34 + 55 = 89

These Fibonacci features
help creatures to survive.
They're part of nature's grand design
to keep each beast alive.

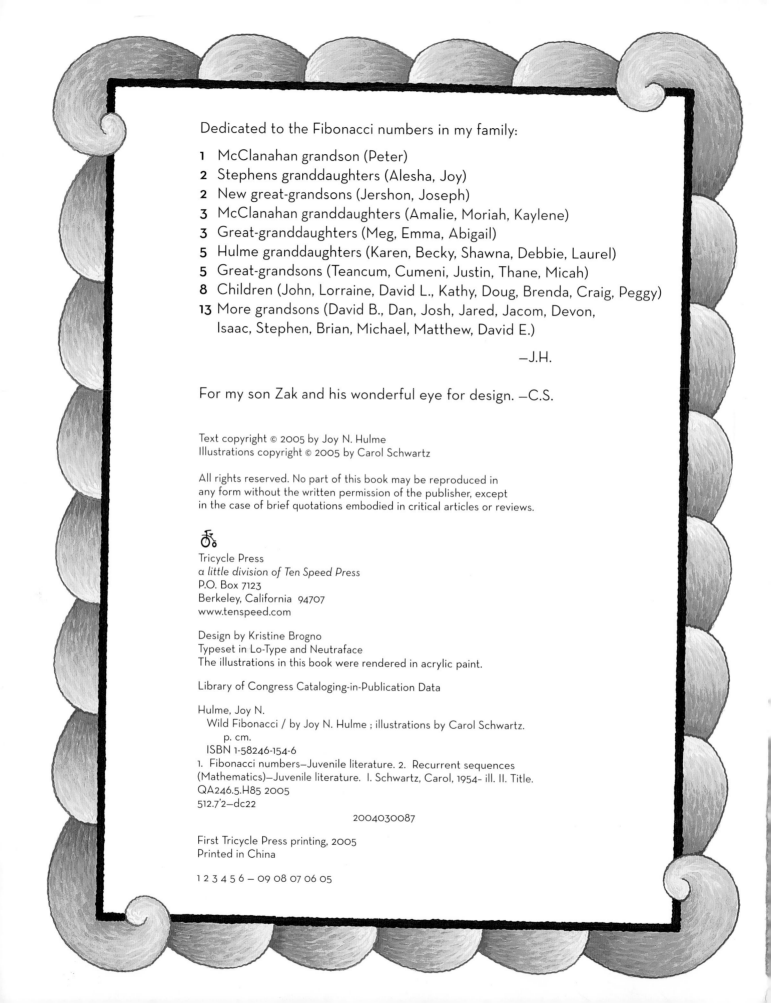

Dedicated to the Fibonacci numbers in my family:

1 McClanahan grandson (Peter)
2 Stephens granddaughters (Alesha, Joy)
2 New great-grandsons (Jershon, Joseph)
3 McClanahan granddaughters (Amalie, Moriah, Kaylene)
3 Great-granddaughters (Meg, Emma, Abigail)
5 Hulme granddaughters (Karen, Becky, Shawna, Debbie, Laurel)
5 Great-grandsons (Teancum, Cumeni, Justin, Thane, Micah)
8 Children (John, Lorraine, David L., Kathy, Doug, Brenda, Craig, Peggy)
13 More grandsons (David B., Dan, Josh, Jared, Jacom, Devon, Isaac, Stephen, Brian, Michael, Matthew, David E.)

—J.H.

For my son Zak and his wonderful eye for design. —C.S.

Text copyright © 2005 by Joy N. Hulme
Illustrations copyright © 2005 by Carol Schwartz

Tricycle Press
a little division of Ten Speed Press
P.O. Box 7123
Berkeley, California 94707
www.tenspeed.com

Design by Kristine Brogno
Typeset in Lo-Type and Neutraface
The illustrations in this book were rendered in acrylic paint.

Library of Congress Cataloging-in-Publication Data

Hulme, Joy N.
   Wild Fibonacci / by Joy N. Hulme ; illustrations by Carol Schwartz.
      p. cm.
   ISBN 1-58246-154-6
1. Fibonacci numbers—Juvenile literature. 2. Recurrent sequences
(Mathematics)—Juvenile literature. I. Schwartz, Carol, 1954- ill. II. Title.
QA246.5.H85 2005
512.7'2—dc22

2004030087

First Tricycle Press printing, 2005
Printed in China

1 2 3 4 5 6 — 09 08 07 06 05